DEATH OF AN AFRICAN VILLAGE

Florence Durrant

Death of an African Village

Author: Florence Durrant

Copyright © Florence Durrant (2022)

The right of Florence Durrant to be identified as author of this work has been asserted by the author in accordance with section 77 and 78 of the Copyright, Designs and Patents Act 1988.

First Published in 2022

ISBN 978-1-915492-14-2 (Paperback)
     978-1-915492-15-9 (E-Book)

Book cover design and Book layout by:
    White Magic Studios
    www.whitemagicstudios.co.uk

Published by:
    Maple Publishers
    1 Brunel Way,
    Slough,
    SL1 1FQ, UK
    www.maplepublishers.com

A CIP catalogue record for this title is available from the British Library.

All rights reserved. No part of this book may be reproduced or translated by any form or by any means, electronic or mechanical, including photocopying, recording or by any information storage and retrieval system without written permission from the author.

The views expressed in this work are solely those of the author and do not necessarily reflect the views of the publisher, and the publisher hereby disclaims any responsibility for them.

CONTENTS

Chapter 1 – The Essence of Life 5

Chapter 2 – African Villages 9

Chapter 3 20

Chapter 4 26

Chapter 5 – My Days in Primary School 32

Chapter 6 – My First Trip to Town 41

Chapter 7 49

Chapter 8 – My Parents 54

There was awesome innocence in me as a child growing up in an African village. A place that was also home to wild and dangerous animals, and as I look back at that childhood an eerie chill runs down my spine. The eerie chill is not one of fear, but rather one inspired by an inexplicable feeling of vulnerability. As I walk back through my journey as a little girl in that village and contrast it with my life as an adult today, I am in awe of how village life was so peaceful and safe, despite the dangers. The innocence I had as a child in that village has now been replaced by the fear of a world full of predators, a world whose safety net is no longer one bound together by a communal spirit of sharing, of love and of respect. It is almost impossible to compare the village life of my childhood to the life I live today. Today that brings back an eerie chill down my spine. That life was a world without electricity, running water, social benefits, clocks or watches, telephones or televisions, not even a radio. Imagine yourself as a six or seven year old tasked with herding your father's cattle, travelling ten kilometres to fetch water, being woken at cockcrow to walk a mile to the field and help your parents with the ploughing or weeding during the planting season. You do an hour or more's work by sunrise, then go back home, wash your face and go to school. After school you return home to continue with the same chores. Nightfall beckons total darkness save for the light of the stars or the once-a-month full moon. Then you sit around a fire listening to some of the best folktales narrated by an imaginative auntie or grandparent; folktales that grip you with such fear you sit transfixed to the spot, holding your bladder and only dare to venture outside accompanied by an adult before retiring for the night, wondering which monster was going to attack you or eat you alive. Despite all this, I have fond memories of that childhood and the love that surrounded me and I hope to bring those memories to life again.

CONTENTS

Chapter 1 – The Essence of Life 5

Chapter 2 – African Villages 9

Chapter 3 20

Chapter 4 26

Chapter 5 – My Days in Primary School 32

Chapter 6 – My First Trip to Town 41

Chapter 7 49

Chapter 8 – My Parents 54

There was awesome innocence in me as a child growing up in an African village. A place that was also home to wild and dangerous animals, and as I look back at that childhood an eerie chill runs down my spine. The eerie chill is not one of fear, but rather one inspired by an inexplicable feeling of vulnerability. As I walk back through my journey as a little girl in that village and contrast it with my life as an adult today, I am in awe of how village life was so peaceful and safe, despite the dangers. The innocence I had as a child in that village has now been replaced by the fear of a world full of predators, a world whose safety net is no longer one bound together by a communal spirit of sharing, of love and of respect. It is almost impossible to compare the village life of my childhood to the life I live today. Today that brings back an eerie chill down my spine. That life was a world without electricity, running water, social benefits, clocks or watches, telephones or televisions, not even a radio. Imagine yourself as a six or seven year old tasked with herding your father's cattle, travelling ten kilometres to fetch water, being woken at cockcrow to walk a mile to the field and help your parents with the ploughing or weeding during the planting season. You do an hour or more's work by sunrise, then go back home, wash your face and go to school. After school you return home to continue with the same chores. Nightfall beckons total darkness save for the light of the stars or the once-a-month full moon. Then you sit around a fire listening to some of the best folktales narrated by an imaginative auntie or grandparent; folktales that grip you with such fear you sit transfixed to the spot, holding your bladder and only dare to venture outside accompanied by an adult before retiring for the night, wondering which monster was going to attack you or eat you alive. Despite all this, I have fond memories of that childhood and the love that surrounded me and I hope to bring those memories to life again.

Chapter 1

The Essence of Life

There are many different stimulus that can trigger forgotten memories: an event, a person, a situation, a specific date or even a thought can activate forgotten memories. Some memories are enjoyable whilst others may be painful. Some memories are treasured, others bring tears of joy to our eyes or make us cry with sadness or laugh with happiness whilst others bring the chill down our spine. In most cases memories may not be felt as intensely as the original experience even though the connection remains there as we revisit them from time to time. In my attempt to revisit my childhood memories, I have battled with many emotions. I believe I am a very philosophical woman: born in dire poverty, I grew up dreaming of a better life for myself and my family. I had long term goals of getting a good education so as to get a good job and help my village out of its poverty. I achieved the first; I worked my way out of poverty to live a fairly comfortable life. However with the death of my mother in 1981, I was forced to re-examine the meaning and purpose of my life. I focussed on helping my village as best as I could but with the death of my father in 2003, that dream also fell apart. A childhood dream that I had nurtured all my life fell apart as I was unable to help my village out of its poverty. Failure to help my village due to the death of both my parents had a huge impact on my philosophy of life. I lost all purpose and meaning to my life forcing me to re visit my lived experience growing up in a little village when I felt my life had a purpose. These memories resurfaced and refused to be forgotten as I battled to find a new meaning to my life. I have pondered about life and its mysteries. I have been in search for a meaningful purpose of my existence. There are different views about the meaning of life or of the way life should be lived. I can genuinely admit that I have failed many times to find a new purpose and meaning for my life and yet no failure stopped me from trying again.

There is a distinction between the life of an individual and a whole community. The meaningfulness of my life in my village wasn't about happiness or personal achievements. It was about the community nurturing, the sharing, and the feeling of safety as a whole community despite the poverty. Growing up in a close knit village I lived a life of a whole rather than my individual life with my individual needs. It was a meaningful life with a meaningful purpose of developing a poor community into one that sustains itself. But once that community disintegrated with the death of my parents, I began to see myself as an individual divorced from the whole, living a comfortable life in the western society without any safety net or nurturing. I had become a successful adult who had developed an identity crisis as I still had that indigenous trait in me, brought on by my childhood memories. I call it indigenous trait rather than indigenous person because I had removed myself from the community that I grew up with. A village in the remote part of the country where everyone knew each other, worked together and socialised together. But I could not remove myself spiritually from that environment despite the fact that I was living an affluent and comfortable life in the UK. I still regarded myself as Florence from Mopaneni (my village) rather than Florence from Kent in the UK. I carry this trait around as I carry my genes and I exhibit it in my behaviour and how I interact with others.

I used to ask myself questions like: What is it that makes indigenous people content with their lives in the jungle, away from western civilization? I have no doubt that I would be the same had I not got the education that took me away from that nomadic lifestyle of pasturing, subsistence farming, forager-farmers, content with life, blended with life around us, relaxed and helpful. It was the only home we knew. That is the trait that bonded me with my village despite enjoying my affluent life thousands of miles away from my village.

Anyone who has suffered any form of crisis, be it financial, personal, professional, interpersonal as in relationship or health goes through or experiences some form of difficulty, an unstable period and sometimes dangerous. My identity crisis was so deep seated that it affected my day to day life and yet I could not get to the bottom of it to explain myself to others. I found myself in a situation I had no control over, and no one understood why I was so driven to re - create that whole indigenous life that shaped my childhood. I felt like a part of me was missing, not just the death of my parents, but the death of my dream, a loss that crippled me for years. I was in my early 40s when my father died taking with him the last dream that I had for my village. And that is when all my childhood memories in my village came flooding back in dreams and nightmares. And yet these memories were based on the first seventeen year of my life. That is why I have revisited my childhood memories, just to tease out that part of me that underpinned my identity crisis after the death of my parents; who am I, what it the meaning and purpose of my life? What is the significance of these dreams and nightmares of a life once lived in a village that is no longer home for me?

Chapter 2

African Villages

African villages differ from one place to the other; from the habitat to their proximity to a major city and other amenities like schools and hospitals. Twenty miles to the north of my village there was a mine compound where locals worked and lived in shacks. It also doubled as the nearest big hospital that provided basic needs of the community. There was also electricity, but I never really got to know the place apart from driving past it. It was another forty miles from the mine to the nearest major city. Ten miles to the south, there was a hospital run by nuns and a secondary school attached to it that was run by priests. They too had electricity. It was where all villagers who had been converted to Roman Catholicism went every Easter to worship the Holy Mary and celebrate the death of her son Jesus Christ. The journey was like a pilgrimage as hundreds of people/worshippers congregated from Friday to Monday, sleeping in tents provided by the church. Two miles from my home was our local primary school. There was no electricity, no running water and pit latrines. That is where I was baptised with the rest of my village children to start our first grade of our primary education; what I now regard as the first stage of indoctrination. Religious indoctrination was the major part of education apart from learning how to read and write. It was when a child was deemed old enough to start school. There was no nursery education and starting school depended on your height and the baptism was a prerequisite for being allowed to start your education. Part of the baptism entailed being given new names that the nuns deemed fit for the individual, hence mine became Florence. All my childhood names became history and Florence stuck until today. One person who was not impressed about my name change was my mother, but she had no say in the matter. It was only at home that I got called by all my other names. Mudengosiba, which means 'being tall because of a feather', was the one my mum used as I was too tall for my age. I never imagined that one day I would see a picture of Shaka Zulu depicting what that name meant.

The beauty of my village in spring always took my breath away. There is no place that I have seen in my travels all over the world that compares to the habitat that surrounded my village – the leafy Mopane trees, the thorny Ceiba and Acasia trees and the magnificent baobab trees to name a few. Wild edible fruit trees were all over my village. Nothing compared to the beauty of the beginning of spring when everything came alive. We had names for everything; carpets of herbaceous vegetation mingled with yellow and purple varieties of grass and the golden dandelion that attracted all sorts of beetles and insects. It was a haven for wild animals and birds – nothing was sweeter than the howling of jackals, the laughing/cackling of hyenas, the hummingbirds, the cooing of doves and many other birds with their different songs.

I have always wondered how and when I developed the memory of who I was growing up in my village. I am talking about that stage when a child emerges from baby talk to comprehensible conversation and is able to interact as a person who identifies herself with other human beings. The explosion of social media has taught us some of the saddest cases of abandoned children who were adopted by animals. There are many such cases but one that stuck in my mind up to today was a little girl who was abandoned by her own parents and for comfort stayed with dogs in their kennels for six years. She was abandoned as a 3 year old toddler and dogs became her family for 6 years. When she was rescued, she had all the characteristics of a dog; she walked on all fours, jumped like a dog, ate like a dog and barked like a dog. Adapting from dog like behaviour to human normality and interacting with other human beings was the most difficult experience for her because normality for her was the behaviour she had learnt in the 6 years living in the kennels with dogs as her family. Despite therapy and all the professional help she was given, her mental capacities at the age of 22 were still those of a child. Those six years in the kennels completely wiped out what ever memory she had of living and interacting with human beings.

I have no clear recollection of when I became aware of myself as a human being. We had pigs, chickens, cows, donkeys, dogs and goats that we interacted with as part of our family. The only difference was that pigs, cows and donkeys had separate enclosures. But the moment/memory I recall very well is when my brother Mike went to school for the first time. He was a few years older than me. I must have been three or thereabouts at the time. I was so distraught because I thought he was not going to come back, I cried and refused to eat until he came back from school. I began to cling to him in the fear that he was going to leave me for good and it took many weeks before I was reassured. Whether I understood what school meant at that age, I don't know. It was like the instinct of a pack of animals - you want to stay together all the time. He would tell me stories about school and when he started to write and read, he would write something down and then read it back to me. Despite having other siblings, I bonded with him the day he went to school for the first time and likewise he became the nurturing brother who protected me. Having a brother like Mike was like having a twin whom I never wanted to be separated from. That was my first episodic memory of bonding with another human being. After his death in 1984 at the age of 30, I lost part of my memories of growing up with this giant I loved and respected.

Nearly everyone in my village was unemployed, had barely any education, they were all peasants whose livestock comprised mostly of a few cows, a few donkeys, sheep, goats and pigs. Their agricultural land depended on the rain where they toiled from sunrise to sunset just to have enough to feed themselves and their families. A few miles away there were farms owned by white farmers – the land was fertile and they had irrigation schemes in case of drought. In case of drought my village depended on one form of aid or another and travelled miles to fetch water. As we got older, my brother promised my parents that if he got educated, he would study agriculture with a view of helping the village. But just like my dream, it never materialised and my fond memories of my brother were reduced to writing journals about him and here is one of them written on the 16th September 2011.

MY BROTHER MIKE – THE LION HEART

He wears his mane with pride, eyes sharp and focussed he sits like a silhouette *against the sunrise and watches everything from a distance. At a distance, the lioness is a shadow of her past pride, a once proud pride, she sits forlorn and broken. The storm has been and gone, branches lie strewed across the jungle, tree trunks a history of what was once a tree and all there is, is a deafening silence. She primes her ears for that vibrating roar – a roar to awaken her feminine instinct of love and nurturing. Memory is a sensory she cannot comprehend; did the storm that ripped them apart happen yesterday or two decades ago, she wanders into that hollow shadow inside her. The shadow that was once full of aspiration and dreams, where once there was a living soul is now echoing with an emptiness that sinks her heart into unequalled darkness. But she cannot despair even though she has no option or plan B. How can she despair, for she made a promise, a promise to herself and that promise cannot be broken? The words came from inside her, as she intensely watched that coffin lowered to rest, her mind eluded her and insanity took over, her eyes lost focus and she never heard the sound of the last shovel. She was listening to a voice, a voice inside her, and the words clear and simple: to avenge for the life of that one lion in her life whose mane made her proud to call him her brother.*

There is so much debris after a storm, floods bring with them some of the most fearsome reptiles and the aftershock is felt for years. The floods fill the hollow shadows, form craters of their own and in them dwell some of the most fearsome creatures. It is only time that restores jungle life. Yet normality eludes the lioness as she sits alone among the debris. She must maintain a sense of calmness and remain alert and focussed to save her sanity. She must be strong, fend for herself and look after herself. Her jaws are strong enough to rip any reptile or creature that threatens her life, but this forest is no longer her home. As she tries to adapt her mind to her new surroundings, the longing and loneliness eat away at her inside and drains her of whatever life she has. But she cannot walk away from this hell hall: what if the lion is somewhere trying to find his way back. So she sits through this gruesome loneliness; there is so much at stake if she upped and left.

To get into the mind of a grieving person, you must understand grief. Some people mourn their loved ones, others grieve; there is a very fine line in between. It is the intensity of both that varies from person to person. This analogy is about me and my brother Mike. Yes I did make a promise to myself to fight for justice for my brother Mike. For years I silently prayed for him, I begged his soul to help me, I retraced our steps growing up together, sang his favourite songs until I drained myself of sanity. I waited and waited, I used my imagination as a way of connecting with his soul, beseeched the spirit world for the soul of the only brother whose soul I truly loved. There was such a strong bond between me and my brother Mike that will never be broken. I think of him as I re live my childhood memories as if we were still growing up together and sharing an unbroken bond. But that village is no longer there and yet memories live forever. I have no doubt that he too would have done the same grieving for me had I died tragically at a young age like he did. As I visit my memories, I am reliving that life we shared together.

The difference between my indigenous childhood and my life today is that we didn't have calendars to mark the beginning or end of the year. Instead we celebrated each season for what it symbolised. The natural world was celebrated as much as the spiritual world. I have no doubt that before the intervention of western influence, the harmony between the natural and the spiritual was fundamental in keeping track of the seasons of the year. The eco system was fundamental to my village not only as the main part of the natural world, but as the healing part of the world, the mother of all living species who was regarded as sacred. There were keepers of this knowledge who passed it on from generation to generation. I was born at the tail end of that knowledge at a time when western influence had taken over and used religion to change how we viewed that knowledge. Anyone who held onto that knowledge was either ostracized or labelled a witch. Those who still held onto the indigenous beliefs were accused by priests and nuns of worshipping the demons. Healers like my grandfather, began to lose their power as the influence of the west overpowered all rationale. Salvation had to be found in churches and western doctrines. My father did hold onto the knowledge passed down by my grandfather but his knowledge was nothing compared to my grandfather's. There is so much I could have learnt from my father, but the brutality that was inflicted on black people by the colonisers dehumanised many of those who held onto their indigenous knowledge. The incompatibilities of indigenous knowledge and religion could not sustain each other. For one to survive, the other had to be destroyed, thus religion was forced upon indigenous people. The brutality of the religious intervention and monitoring of our lives by the Roman Catholic Church meant many indigenous folks chose survival by accepting religion. As far as I am aware, after my father said goodbye to this world, that knowledge was lost in to the void, irretrievable.

My indigenous status is something I hold dear and yet I feel impotent as to how to retrieve it. My assumption is that being an indigenous person takes more than having the knowledge that my grandfather and my father had. My belief is that, as an indigenous woman, I am more than what religion teaches me, more than what science teaches me, more than what physics teach me and more than the knowledge of the healing plants my grandparents used. I feel strongly that there is a need for an indigenous input in today's hostile society we live in whereby the natural world and the spiritual world are either denied or destroyed.

Parents are pivotal in every child's life. Before religion indoctrinated me with the god vs. devil delusion, I regarded my parents as my gods. They provided for us, protected us, told us what to do, praised us if we did right and disciplined us if we did wrong. They taught us right from wrong with no image of what right or wrong looked like. Grandparents, parents, uncles, aunties and all village elders were respected and every adult had the right to discipline any child for wrongdoing. If they didn't clip your ears, they dragged you to your parents for them to discipline you. Adults had their own hierarchy and they treated each other with respect. Women played the matriarchal duty of looking after the community and were the most likely to discipline children whereas men were providers who either worked in the mines or did most of the farming. There were no locks in our doors and they were no thieves either. Every village respected the property of the other.

Death of an African Village

I cannot place a specific moment in my childhood when my episodic memory with my parents started. However, as I became aware of my family unit, I observed the bonding of the structural hierarchy of my family unit. We lived in a big kraal, a traditional African village of huts, typically enclosed by a fence. At the head of the family were my paternal grandfather and his many wives. All his married sons and their own wives occupied the section of the kraal next to their mother. I have a very vague memory of my paternal grandmother apart from the fact that she was a light skinned woman who was softly spoken. As children we slept with my grandmother in her little hut that was near my grandfather's hut. I recall that my grandfather held many celebrations aimed at appeasing his ancestors and my grandmother as the first wife, took charge of brewing umqomboti, the African beer, as was the tradition. With the death of my grandmother, that family unit split and despite his placid nature, my father always blamed his mother's death on the jealousy she was subjected to by some of my grandfather's other wives. After my grandmother died, all the married sons moved out and built their own little kraals, hence my memories of my little village in Mopaneni are based on the home my parents built after splitting from my grandfather.

What captures my indigenous spirit is that, without calendars, without dates and without time, we lived peacefully and everything blended together perfectly. For instance, my birth would be associated with the season when I was born and not the calendar year; for example, my birth would be marked the year of the flood, the year of bumper harvest, the year of drought etc. Any child born during the same season would be my age despite of who was born first or last. These were my childhood friends

I grew up surrounded by, playing with, herding cattle together, fetching water and firewood together. The loyalty between us meant that we all protected each other. We parted ways after completing primary school, but we all knew what happened to each other. At the age of 12 I made my first virgin journey to start secondary education at a boarding school that was over a hundred miles from my village. But I always met up with my friends at Christmas time. Nothing beat the pleasure of that reunion, which was about old friends getting together as if we had never parted ways. But between the timespan of my episodic memory to the end of my childhood in my village, we lived what I would only sum up as supreme blessedness in our little paradise of indigenous life. At the age of 14 most of my childhood friends went to work in town as house maids, a few got married to local boys whilst I continued with my student days at boarding school. Even then there was no competition, we were just village friends with a village mentality of giving back the little we had to our parents and relatives, working together in the field and fetching water together.

Not one of them is alive today. Poverty and disease are intertwined. If you are poor, you are destined to die like a pauper, no medical intervention of any sort and only those close to you feel the pain. That is what gave birth to the dream I had before my father died; to help build a little clinic in his home with a view of focussing on health promotion. I have been a nurse for over 30 years and health promotion has always been central to my nursing. I wanted to use this knowledge to help my village because most of them contracted HIV and didn't believe that it was sexually transmitted. That dream wasn't a success for the simple fact that there was no one in my village to honestly work with resulting in a loss of my money that I had invested for that purpose. In 2011, I found out that my father's home had become a ghost home after the death of my step mother in 2007. Despite the disappointment, this was a catalyst I needed to end that connection with my village both spiritually and physically. I have absolutely no doubt that even if I visited my village, no one will recognise me. That is why revisiting my childhood memories has become the only way to connect with the community of a close knit family that was once my home.

Chapter 3

In my village, nothing broke night into dawn more sharply than the crowing of roosters and their timing was like clockwork. On a normal day, that would mean getting up and starting some chores. In this chapter, I will focus on the busiest time of the year, beginning of spring to the end of summer. The first rains after winter start around September/October and they are called imbolisamahlanga, which means the rains that rot the old chaff, the old stalk from the previous harvest. This was the beginning of the planting season and in my village we used both cows and donkeys to pull the plough. Three people were needed in most cases, one to lead the cows/donkeys pulling them in a straight line, the other walked behind the cows planting seeds and the third held the plough. The best time to plough was first thing in the morning before it got too hot. As a young child, this was the most strenuous job yet it was expected of us as soon as our parents deemed that we were old enough to help out with such chores.

Everyone who was old enough to partake in the ploughing chores was awoken at the crowing of the rooster by either my mother or father and the simple sentence of "Vukani bantwabami/wake up children" sent shivers down my spine and I was known to cry with grief for my sleep, begging to be allowed to sleep for a little while longer. Subsequently, I was referred to as the lazy one and apparently I was also very good at faking some illness of one form or the other. But it never worked. The older siblings would get the cows/donkeys and the plough ready, just as one would with horse-drawn carriage. We were all allocated chores on daily basis, so if it was my turn, I would go the fields to lead the cows whilst my brother walked behind them and one of my parents holding the plough in place. It was done in such a way that made sure the depth of the plough was adequate enough to cover the seeds. Just after sunrise we would be sent home to get ready for school.

Water was very scarce unless it was the rainy season. We had a well in the field that filled up only during the rainy season and it was used by everyone who lived within our vicinity. If the well was empty, it meant walking five miles to the only borehole that supplied the whole village of over twenty families. Imagine a 5 year old girl who had been walking bare foot leading cows in either a dusty or muddy field for over an hour. You had to go back home, wash your face and legs and go to school. That was the reality that I lived. I would carry my little bucket and with my mother we would fetch water from the well, go back home and my mother/auntie would help me wash my face and my feet. We would have porridge made out of maize or sorghum and then run to school. Lateness was not tolerated and if you were late you got clubbed. We would finish school around 12 pm; go back home and then start another round of chores. Between the ages of 5 to 7 years, we would be sent on some small errands if there were any and then meet up with our friends to play. This was normal for every child in my village. It did not matter where we were playing; we knew when to go back home by where the sun was.

We understood the importance of time keeping as other chores awaited us at home and every child was at home before sunset. The chores that we did at that age ranged from helping whoever was herding the animals to round them up, and herd the goats and sheep into their own enclosures and cows into their shed. There were other little chores that had to be done before sunset, like helping my mother or auntie collect firewood before they cooked dinner. Dinner, which was our main meal, was the acclaimed "paps", a thickened porridge eaten with vegetables or other condiments like "amasi" which is fermented milk or "amacimbi" - the Mopani caterpillar. Meat was a rarity and when we had chicken, children always had the basic, maybe just one piece that we had to share and the head, neck and legs. We all shared whatever we had as everything was rationed. That was all we knew, so we were content with what we were given. That was the other reason why spring was awesome in many ways. Wild fruit was plentiful in spring and complimented our diet. Goats and cows were having babies and we got a lot of milk from them too. That cycle of ploughing happened every year after the first rains.

The field was a large area of land and all my grandfather's sons shared the land. We called this land field not farm. Farming was a term used to describe white people who owned land for commercial farming, whereas in our case it was for family sustenance. Each family had their own path they used to walk through their field into different parts of their land where a variety of crop was planted. The main crops were maize, different varieties of sorghum, water melon, pumpkins, different types of nuts, sweet potatoes and a different kind of sugarcane which is much softer that the common hard sugarcane. The land was divided between my father and his brother by my grandfather and there were no fences separating the land. The division was marked by an uncultivated strip of land which was roughly two feet wide and stretched from one family's path to the next family. But we could all roam wherever we wanted and our parents talked to each whilst doing the chores in the field.

There was one man who owned a tractor and his home was five miles away from ours. He was also in charge of the borehole where we went to fetch water. He had trained as an agricultural officer and also doubled as a veterinary. I don't recall exactly what he did as we didn't vaccinate our animals. Whenever my father could afford, he would hire him just to cultivate the land and then we would plant seeds afterwards. This took so much pressure off my parents as the planting had to be done on time if we wanted to get a good crop. We always waited for him to finish so that we could get a lift to fetch water from the borehole. We used to love it and always found the ride enjoyable as this was the only type of vehicle we rode in our childhood. The road was bumpy and the side to side movement /the swaying movement/rocking movement of the trailer was so much fun we would talk about it for days on end.

When the ploughing and sowing was done, we waited in anticipation for the seeds to germinate. Whoever saw the first seed ran back home to tell everyone. It was such a novelty for my child's mind to imagine how a hard seed can break itself underground in total darkness and force its way out of the ground to become a seedling. I used to believe that the ritual my village did of appeasing the ancestors was responsible for the germination. Before ploughing season, my father and his brothers and other local villagers each took a basket full of seeds to my grandfather who performed the ritual of appeasing the ancestors in a celebration where elders drank umqomboti and danced their traditional dance until the early hours of the morning. After germination, my paternal grandfather and other local elders went to Matopo's Hill and spent seven days in Njelele, the rain making shrine praying to uNkulunkulu for rain. They took umqomboti with them which served as an offering to uNkulunkulu and ancestors and it was poured on the ground at the entrance of the cave.

The rainmaking shrine was revered by people all over Matebeleland. The belief was that uNkulunkulu once lived there. This deity has different names and yet is understood to be one and the same deity. Other names used in Matebeleland are uThixo and uMlimu. They believed that this deity was the creator of the world, the highest authority behind their ancestors. To call Njelele a cave is understating its complexity. It is a gallery of rocks with hidden entrances and small tunnels which lead to the shrine's various chambers. The story is that there were cult priests who had access to these chambers and that no one was allowed to visit Njelele without the presence of a traditional priest. The priest or priestess was also the custodian of the shrine. My paternal grandfather and other village elders were the intermediaries because they were the people who understood this culture, were well versed in this tradition and revered this deity. This creator was believed to have powers to provide adequate rain for agricultural and livestock prosperity, and it was also believed that this deity spoke to the intermediaries before they left the shrine.

These ceremonies were very impressive to me. I just loved the whole atmosphere of celebration, eating, dancing and community spirit. I had no idea then the impact religion would have on me, the indoctrination by the Roman Catholic. How their rituals were totally different from ours. This communication with this deity and the spiritual world of my grandfather continued to make me question religion even when my conviction in Christian beliefs got stronger. The difference between the deity worshipped by the Roman Catholic and the deity that was revered by my grandparents is that the Roman Catholic had a name and gender of this god as Jesus Christ whilst my grandparents revered a deity that had no gender and was called uNkulunkulu/UMlimu. Even though my grandparents went to speak to this deity in the cave in Matopo's Hill, their deity was a totality of the cosmos. It is now commonly known as African Spirituality but it could easily pass as Pantheism, this reverence, awe, wonder, respecting nature and active care for the right of all humans and living beings. This is what I carried on as part of my being rather than as a religious belief. Thankfully, my father continued with this ritual until I was old enough to make an informed decision on which one to choose.

Chapter 4

My father always spoke about how his father's spirit was crushed when he was forced to leave his home at the foot of Matopo's hill. In the words of Miriam Makeba, "When we speak about people in Southern Africa we have to be specific, there are two separate communities, that is the white communities and black communities. The white men, whether in the majority or the minority always rules; when they came to us, we welcomed them and gave them seats, they sat down. Once they were comfortable, they told us to get up and that is how they conquered and they ruled." There is a lot written about what Miriam Makeba says, but one book sums it all up in this quote: "The origin of apartheid is conquest, slavery and racism. Whites systematically oppressed, dominated and exploited blacks. Over decades, a powerful minority enforced injustice through political structures that coerced the majority of citizens into poverty stricken, second-class, segregated conditions." Hennie Lotter. That is how my grandfather was forced to move from his village and forced to settle 70 miles away from KwaBulawayo. They were forced from their homes under a scheme called Reservations. Reserving the land and they chose places that were fertile or sacred to the indigenous people. Men like my grandfather lost all their livestock and whatever little belonging they had as soon as Cecil John Rhodes conquered their leader King Lobengula.

Death of an African Village

As I grew older, I battled to understand why my grandfather was forced to leave his home and why that broke his heart. But no one really talked about it in detail. My maternal grandmother, who came to live with us in her later years used to tell us some of the most harrowing stories. One that I remember very well was her experience as a young girl. She was sitting in her field shelling nuts when two white men on horseback approached her. She had already been warned by her parents to run away if a white man approached her. She was so frightened she could not even move and, semi paralysed she wet herself. When they started talking to her, she couldn't understand what they were saying and the only thing she could think of was that they were looking for her parents. So she started mumbling, unable to speak properly and tried to give them directions to her home. After they left her, she couldn't remember how long they had been there or what they did to her. All she remembered was that she was never the same after that experience, unable to go anywhere alone. She would say with a distant look as if looking into that day and say, "Something in me died that day."

Hennie P. P. Lötter describes exactly what my grandmother's experienced when she had first contact with those two white men: "This segregated system harmed not only blacks, but also whites. Blacks lost their freedom, their lives and their sense of self-esteem; whilst whites suffered a breakdown in moral equity and a deprivation of cultural diversity." My grandparents experienced first-hand what Lötter wrote, but they could not write their history down for future generations to know the truth. So they passed the little they could to us in whatever way or form they could muster. Their land was stolen from them under the scheme of reservations

– reserving the best land for white entrepreneurs from all over Europe who were lured to Africa by its richness in resources, habitat, wild animals and trusting indigenous people. Not only were they forced out of their land, their livestock was stolen from them and they were told where to settle. The mastermind of this stealth was Cecil John Rhodes and this was how he justified this robbery: "I contend that we are the first race in the world, and that the more of the world we inhabit the better it is for the human race." He had absolutely no regard for indigenous black people as he saw them not fit for their land and I quote him again; "I prefer land to Negros." That is what broke my grandfather's spirit and the whole black indigenous communities that were colonised and enslaved.

My grandfather died when I was still very young, but I still do remember him as a very authoritative man who commanded respect from all his wives and other villagers. His hut stood alone at the front of all other huts. There were always people coming and going who I suspect came to him with ailments they wanted him to treat. I also gathered from my father that he was a very generous man and that many people who settled in our village came from different parts of the country having been displaced from their homes to make way for reservations and reserves.

Something about my childhood is that I somehow held onto these stories wondering whether I could do something to make my parents proud of me. Until the age of 12 my life just revolved around my village. I didn't even know where Matopo Hill was or how it looked like. I had never been to any town or knew anything about electricity. Our connection with other places was the bus which took people to and from Bulawayo. I cannot remember which day it travelled, but it went past our home very early in the morning to Bulawayo, picking people along the way. Some people were travelling to the compounds of the mine or to Bulawayo in search of work. But they were many who used the bus to visit relatives in other parts of Matebeleland. The same bus made its return journey later on in the day and to us that was a novelty, some fun to look forward to; just standing by the roadside waving at the driver and passengers. If we were lucky the driver would throw us a packet of sweets that we shared among ourselves. The roads were dusty roads so whenever we ran behind the bus, we would be covered in dust. Once in a while someone would alight at the bus stop that my father made. It was usually some auntie or uncle working in town or the mines, but there were very few people from my village working in town and they worked either as nannies or garden boys earning pittance. They always made the end of month visit to their families with little amount of groceries they could afford.

My childhood up to the age of 12 had absolutely no understanding of the realities of life. Poverty was relative as everyone was the same in my village; all dependent on their agricultural harvest. I don't remember the first time there was drought, where most crops were scorched before harvest. But it was so bad that the whole of Matebeleland was in danger of starving. Later in his life, my father would recall the year when he cried for his father and all the elders who used to go and pray for rain in Matopo Hill. According to my father, the ones who were doing the rituals after my grandfather died were no longer the real cultural priests left from Logengula's legacy. He blamed it all on the creation of the reservations that saw white people take over the land around Matopo Hill forcing indigenous people into settlements whilst claiming the land to be theirs. The relevance of that was that Matopo Hill was no longer sacred to the indigenous folks. "No spirit of our ancestors would allow something like this to happen." he would say. In his own mind, the spirit was angry and therefore abandoned us. That was the drought that killed many people in the whole of Matebeleland. Villagers depended on the donation of corn meal from some Christian Aid and other government schemes.

As I grew older, I do remember subsequent droughts in my village. Some families including mine did have a little bit of harvest to see them through to the next one. It didn't matter how little my parents harvested, my mother always made sure that there was something in store to feed us one meal per day. However, if my mum heard that a child in the neighbourhood hadn't eaten for days, she would make me take my one meal to feed that child. Apart for a few years, my parents always did have a fairly good harvest. Hence many poor families looked up to my mother when their children had nothing to eat. The family with poor harvest depended on the generosity of their neighbours. It was this grounding that made me admire my mother and dreamt of helping my village on a larger scale.

Harvest time was the most festive time of the year for everyone in my village. The festive was celebrated in gratitude to the spirit of my fore parents and to appease ancestors. Each of my grandfather's sons and unmarried adult daughters collected their first harvest and gave them to my grandfather. This was then followed by the harvest festival where everyone gathered at my grandfather's home. There was always umqomboti, a lot of dancing and singing, drinking and eating and my grandfather would bless the harvest and perform the ritual of pouring some umqomboti on the ground. This ritual was meant to quench the thirst of his ancestors. As children we loved this period of plenty. All in all, it made the hard work of ploughing worth enduring. It was not only a season for plenty for humans, but livestock as well were well fed. After the death of my grandfather, my father continued with this ritual until he died in 2003. I still miss these rituals and no amount of dancing in church can bring that feel good factor that I felt during the African ancestral celebrations. Looking back, I believe those ancestral celebrations connected me to this cosmos or universal god rather than the euphoria one gets in dancing in fellowship in church making me continue to yearn for them. Now I regard my belief in this deity as a spiritual belief and I don't look for god in churches or religion, but I look for godly act in all living things.

Chapter 5

My Days in Primary School

From the early 1980s some of the villagers and relatives had converted to Christianity and regarded my ancestral celebration as worshipping demons. This was the religious teachings according to the Roman Catholic. However, despite her Christian beliefs, my mother participated in my father ancestral rituals. She is the one who was responsible for brewing umqomboti and the cooking of food. But she didn't actively participate in the celebrations themselves. I cannot remember a time when I ever questioned my father's cultural beliefs even though I had also become a zealous Christian after starting boarding school at the age of 12. Even as an adult living in the UK, those yearly visits to my village for my father to perform this ritual filled with me with delight and elation. The proof of how important these celebrations were to me is that I felt lost without my yearly visits to my village after my father's death. I didn't understand that strong impact these celebration were on my life until I had this feeling of being disconnected from everything as if I was confined in some solitary planet of my own secluded from the rest of the world.

My local school was called St Anna's school and it was a lower primary school that provided education for children for the first five years of their education. It was built by the Roman Catholic and was designed to teach local children how to read and write whilst being indoctrinated with Catholicism. The classes were divided into five classes - Sub A, Sub B, Grade 1, Grade 2 and Grade 3. There were only 3 classrooms that we shared in rotas, meaning that some children had to be taught outside, sitting under a tree apart from during the winter months whereby Sub A and Sub B classes finished early making room for the higher grades. There were different kinds of outdoor activities that freed the classes for other grades, mainly PE, gardening and fetching water for school use from a well that was five miles away. I don't recall much of my days at that school apart from weekly religious studies. White nuns made their weekly visit from the Catholic Church that was ten miles away to teach these lessons. On Sunday, the priest accompanied them to Sunday mass. All the teachers were male, black and local. They were all devout Catholics. They were revered by the villagers for their occupation. One of them was my cousin whose home was next to ours. His mother was my father's sister. They obtained their one year teaching qualification from a Roman Catholic school in Bulawayo, apart from the Head teacher who was educated in a Catholic missionary school in Mashonaland. Any parent who had aspirations for their children wanted them to be teachers. However, many children never continued with their education after Grade 3. I believe that one of the reasons was that the upper primary schools that offered Grade 4 and 5 were ten miles away from our village. There were also school fees to be paid to attend these upper primary schools and very few parents could afford them.

The Roman Catholic school that offered upper primary was called St Joseph's school and it was predominantly run by nuns and the priests. But my parents could not afford the fees. My mother's denomination was the Salvation Army and she was dedicated to her church. Like all other local churches, hers also had a school that was built by the church. The school also offered upper primary education to local children. After finishing my lower primary education, I had no idea what was to become of me. I also stopped going to church on Sunday at my local school. Instead I went with my mother to her church a few times. When the school term started my parents didn't have any money to pay for my fees at St Josephs. The first month of the school term I stayed at home herding my father's livestock. I believed then that my fate was sealed and I would either end up getting married at the age of 14 or be forced to go to look for work as a nanny in Bulawayo. I cried every day and my mother was equally in despair. My dear mother would pray every night for someone to help her and one day she promised me that she would get me back to school. I knew she had no money and my father wasn't going to help her. My father's reasoning was that girls didn't need any further education once they were able to read and write. He had been angered by my eldest sister, the first born who got pregnant and failed to finish her nurse training in Zambia.

It was a Wednesday, a month after the school term started and my mother had attended women's meeting at her church. I had spent most of the day herding my father's goats. When she got back that evening, she was very excited and started talking to my father. She had not only secured me a place to go back to school, but her cousin who was the head teacher of Lingwe School, the school that doubled as her church had given her some money for my school fees. The school fees were not more than £3 in those days, but it was a lot for most villagers. I have no recollection whatsoever of how I felt from that day until I went to Lingwe school. I later found out that my father wasn't pleased because it meant hiring a local boy to herd his goats.

My mother cycled to her church because it was very far from our home. For someone of my age, it meant walking for over an hour just to get to school. The first day I left home before dawn and I walked alone until sun rise. I was late for school and the head teacher was not happy. He asked me to tell my mother that I was late for school and in future I would be punished. For a few weeks I left home whilst it was still dark and travelled alone. One day I caught up with some pupils who lived a couple of miles from my home and it felt so good to travel with others. I told my mother when I got home and from that day on, I woke up even earlier to catch up with them. At the end of the term I was so tired my mother suggested to my father that she could arrange for me to stay with some of her friends who lived near the school. My mother worked her magic again and his cousin, the head teacher allowed me to stay with him in the staff accommodation. He was already staying with two of his nieces and the three of us shared the little round hut that doubled as a kitchen. I soon found out that this kind cousin of my mother was not only strict at school, but he was worse at home.

I had never cooked paps, our staple food until I stayed with the head teacher. The first few days, his niece who was older did the cooking and I did the washing up just as I had done at home. Then he made us take turns in cooking and I did a booboo. He threw his paps on the ground, shouted at me for wasting his mealie meal and then I got his belt on my back. The next morning in class he asked all the girls whether they know how to cook paps. They were a few who did and others who didn't. He told all those who didn't know that we were all stupid and needed some beating. We all got the belt and it was the second time for me. I later found out that his niece who was older than me also went through the same treatment. That Sunday I waited for mother to tell her of this hell. I could only speak to her after church. But as I went to her with tears in my eyes, I could see the head teacher's eyes penetrating through me. He was a respected man as the head teacher and was doing me and my mother a favour.

My maternal grandmother and the head teacher's mother were sisters whereas his nieces where his sister's children. If he could treat his first nieces with such brutality, what chances did I stand? So I swallowed my tears and greeted my mother and told her everything was all right. The head teacher expected the best from all his pupils and he reigned with terror on other teachers when their pupils didn't get good grades. He was younger than most of the teachers, but they all treated him like a god. He was feared by both teachers and pupils alike. I remember him as always immaculately dressed. He walked around the school with a pen in one hand and a stick in the other. I spent the first year in a haze and at the age of 10, my life completely changed from being a spoilt poor village girl to a studious obedient girl. I also learnt how to cook paps, wash my uniform and clean his hut and the kitchen. The highlight of my life was being allowed to visit home at the week-end at the end of each month. At the end of term, I went home for the holidays and told my mother the nightmare that I was going through. She gave me a choice;

finish my upper primary school so as to go to secondary school or leave school and herd my father's goats. His two nieces were not treated any different from me. The older niece was a class ahead of me and therefore finished her upper secondary school at the end of the year.

My second and final year at Lingwe School staying with my mother's cousin was the worst nightmare. His older niece was no longer there to do most of the chores and therefore he expected me to do all the chores. One day we were given some homework to do after school. After school, I and his niece went to fetch water and when we got back it was already getting dark. So we did our homework first as there was no electricity, and then we were going to cook paps after we had finished our homework. The head teacher always went to the local store for a few beers after school - (later would marry the woman who worked there as cashier). As I and his niece were doing our homework in the kitchen, he walked in furious that we had not cooked paps for him. I told him that we were doing the homework that he had given us. Both of us got a good clubbing and he was so angry he told us not to cook anything. We went to bed hungry. It was obvious that he was drunk. At the week-end I took all my belongings and ran away. I couldn't go home because I knew my mother would be angry. So I wandered around until dark and slept under a tree a few miles from my home. It did the trick for me. Once the head teacher found out that I had left, he cycled to my home to check if I was there. That is when the search team went looking for me everywhere. When I finally got the courage to go home in the morning, my mother was beside herself. That is when I told her of the beatings we endured from his cousin. I still had the bruises from the beatings, my mother believed me. But what choice did she have?

I know my father wasn't happy about it and wanted me not to go back to my uncle, the brutal head teacher. I recall my mother giving me a choice, to get up at crack of dawn or stay with my uncle. I did go back to stay with the head teacher and I was allowed to visit home every other week-end. My mother came to her church twice a week, on Wednesdays and Sundays. This time round I felt more comfortable because I knew that she would always check up on me. A few things changed after that. The after school beatings from the head teacher for not doing chores like cooking on time or cleaning his round hut properly stopped. He started openly dating his cashier girlfriend and brought her over to his round hut. She was a sweet woman who embraced us as an older sibling does. She sometimes brought us some sweets. I later found out that it was my mother who had convinced his cousin, the young man who was sort after by many village young ladies, to settle down with this cashier woman. It worked like magic as she did most of the cooking and we were no longer required to clean his bedroom. He became kinder to us and I have no doubt that it was because he was also happy in himself.

I have vague memories of my last day at that school. I was convinced that I had failed my final exams. I was 12 years of age then and I knew I had two choices; pass my exams or herd my father's cows until I turned 14 and got married for dowry. What I remember is that my mother told me that if I passed my exams, his cousin had agreed to lend her the $10, the deposit that was required to be accepted at the boarding school that I had applied to. I don't recall personally applying for a place to start my secondary education. Therefore have no doubt that my mother asked his cousin to apply for me. What I do remember is that one Sunday my mother came back from church and she looked at me with sad eyes. I knew she had got my results. So I started crying only for her to burst out singing her favourite song; "Themba kuThixo ohlezi kuye" Trust your god where you are sitting or trust your god who owns you. She had tears in her eyes as she opened the envelope for me. I had straight As in all subjects. That was the part of my childhood that made me bond with my mother in a spiritual manner. How can a woman sacrifice so much for me? That is when I decided that I would do everything to make up for what she did for me. Sadly, I never did as she died in In October 1981, the month I got my first job, a young woman in her early 50s, she said goodbye to this world having suffered a stroke that paralysed her for the three weeks before she died.

I was 21 years old when my mother died. It took a long time for me to realise that I am no exception when it comes to bereavement; it happens to most of us. But how do we react so differently to grief; what do some people feel so lost or feel so alone when this world is full of people? If there was a stairway to follow that one could climb to follow a deceased relative, I would have followed my mother. That is how much grief stricken I was. The death of my mother paralysed me for many year until I had counselling in 1998. I was paralysed spiritually rather than physically because I was physically functioning normally, building my career and travelling all over the world. I was sad not depressed, the emptiness was inside me. I yearned for that part of my life when I had dreams about helping my mother and my village. Despite visiting my village every year to connect with my village people, the absence of my mother was like a burden in my heart. My father remained the rock that connected me to my village and yet I couldn't talk to him about how I felt, so I carried that burden until my father died in 2003. His death marked the end of my visits to my village and I stopped identifying myself as Florence from Mopaneni.

By the age of 25, with both my brother Mike and my mother were dead, I felt like they had taken with them the dream that I had for my village. I had to rethink about the meaning of my life and my identity. A year later, I left Zimbabwe and came to England where I trained as a nurse. For the first ten years of my life in England, I focussed on my career and I became successful both in my career and my personal life. I also made a great network of likeminded friends and I settled down in married life bringing up my son and working hard in my endeavour to have a comfortable home and a comfortable life. Yet I carried around me this burden that stopped me from enjoying my life away from my village. There is a word that describes people like me: indigenous; because the history of our village and how we came to live there was passed from our grandparents and our parents after them making it part of us. It is not the same as buying a house because the house carries the memories of the previous owners. We were an ethnic group who inhabited a geographic region with which we have the earliest known historical connection. I suspect therefore that this feeling of the heavy burden was caused by the loss of the matriarch who made all the decision in our home. Despite living in the UK for over two decades and having a successful career I still carried that indigenous trait that made me feel incomplete and lost. The memories of my childhood refused to go away as I capture them in this book.

Chapter 6
My First Trip to Town

I was 12 years of age when I went to a boarding school that was far away from my home. To get to the boarding school, I travelled by bus to Bulawayo, 70 miles from my home so as to connect with another bus that took us to our boarding school. I still remember that day vividly because I never slept the whole night in fear of missing the bus. We had no watch or a radio to tell us the time except that we knew that the bus arrived at our stop just after sunrise. There was only one bus per day travelling to Bulawayo and so as not to miss that bus, my mother accompanied me to the bus stop before sunrise. My emotions were mixed, a combination of excitement and dreading what lay ahead. But I had worked so hard to pass my exams and also seen how hard my mother had worked to get me where I was – ready for boarding school.

Having a daughter go to boarding school was a novelty in my village. All the correspondence came through the head teacher at Lingwe School. He is the one who sent the names of the best achievers and his word was final. With the letter of acceptance, the school sent an inventory for all first year students of what to bring with them, bedsheets, pillowcases, nightdress and underpants. My parents could not afford to buy any of them. But what was most important was that my mother had the $10 that was required as entrance fees. The rest was a collaborative effort between my aunties who made me underpants, nightdress and pillows from the pieces of material they collected from what was left from my father's sewing business. I only had one bedsheet from the material my father bought. One of my aunties made me two pairs of underpants and the rationale was that at the end of the day I would wash one and wear the other and by the following morning I would wash the one I wore and wear the one I washed the previous day.

My father bought me a metal trunk, a requirement that was on the acceptance letter. It was small but after packing everything I had, it was still barely half full. I had never travelled by bus before and there was only one bus service to town per week from my village. My mother woke me up at the crack of dawn and she accompanied me to the bus stop. She gave me the instructions of where to go once I got to town. I had to stay with her sister who worked as a nanny for a white family. She lived with her family, 4 people living in a two bedroom rented house at the location called Mzilikazi, one of many densely populated locations for black people in Bulawayo. I stayed with them until the day I connected with the bus that took us to our boarding school, 50 or so miles from Bulawayo. I had never met that auntie before as she never visited us in the village. She was the first born in my mother's family and my mother was the third born. I carried my trunk from the bus stop looking for my auntie's address. Her house was not very far from the bus terminal, but it took me more than an hour to find it. When I knocked at the door, I was met by an indifferent cousin who greeted me as her cousin from the country. Her mother had asked her to wait for me and she complained that I had taken a long time to arrive as she wanted to go and play with her friends. The following day I went to find a Salvation Army church near the bus terminal where another bus would take me to my boarding school. My cousin who was my age refused to accompany me. In her words "she was embarrassed to be seen with a relative from the village". I must have been the first to arrive at this church as there was an empty bus waiting to take us to Usher Girl's Secondary school. Many other girls seemed as completely lost as I was. Others had relatives accompanying them. But we all cheered up once we got onto the bus and started talking to each other. That was the beginning of the four years that turned me from a village girl with a bible in her hand to one who questioned the bible.

Upon arrival we were ushered into dormitories and mine had 20 single beds with just a mattress, a blanket and a pillow without a pillow case. As we unpacked, I watched as other girls began to unpack their bed sheets and pillows from the plastic coverings. Some still had prize tags attached. My bedsheet and pillow cases that were made for me by my auntie were just crushed in my trunk. I was aware that some of the girls were looking at me and laughing. For me the novelty of just making it to secondary school outweighed my poverty. I soon blended in with other girls and made friends with a few. There were other girls who did not have bedsheets and they looked embarrassed. My poverty soon became negligible as we started classes and made friends with girls from other dormitories. I recall my first friend Lucy. Her parents worked at the farm where our school was built. Her uncle was the cook for the school. That friendship continued for four years and I visited her home that was a couple of miles from school. Her parents were very poor too but they were very kind.

The school was built on a land owned by a white farmer. The land was very big and the school was fenced around and there was a large space around the buildings where we used to go and sit during our spare time. The farmer had a big house a mile or so from the school. He grew maize and had lots of cattle and sheep. My friend Lucy told me that her grandparents were moved out of that land and settled a few miles away. Her grandparents and her parents worked for the farmer who had moved them out of their own homes. At that age I don't think she really understood why they were moved. I too didn't understand why my grandfather was moved from his home near Matopo hill and settled 70 miles away. We were both from very poor families and grateful to have an education.

Most of my early memories at boarding school are now vague. But the regime from day one was always the same – the bell rang for us to get up in the morning. We lined up for the toilet and the shower and we had to be all dressed up in uniform before the bell rang for us to go for breakfast. After breakfast we went to classes. There were activities after school until the bell rang for supper. After supper we went back to class for study period from 7 - 9 pm. We were supposed to be in bed by 10pm. The nuns patrolled our dormitories checking on anyone who was still awake. If you were caught with your eyes opened you got punished the following day. However, I missed my mother so much that I had occasional nights when I just couldn't sleep. One night I had my eyes opened when the nun's touch hovered around. She had tiptoed into the dormitory and turned on her torch and suddenly there was this flurry of girls covering their faces. I just closed my eyes and pretended to be asleep. Those who were seen covering their heads were punished the following day.

There was a swimming pool that was mainly used by the nuns and students were only allowed to swim as part of PE. I have no recollection of how students were picked for particular sports – I was picked for netball. I had never done any proper swimming apart from playing in our local river and therefore had no interest in swimming. Older girls used to go and swim during the night to cool down in summer as their dormitories were not inspected. Others used to go and hide behind the swimming pool walls to catch up on their revision. In my second year a few girls from my class decided to do the same. I joined them with a view of just revising for my exams. After an hour of revision the girls jumped into the swimming pool to cool down, reluctant as I was, I followed and instead of easing myself in from the shallow end I jumped into the deep end and I had to be rescued as was I drowning. I never went back to the swimming pool again.

On Saturdays, we did chores around the school and cleaned our dormitories and we took turns in cleaning the church. We were not allowed to leave the school premises without permission. During our spare time most of us used to wander around the school complex and several times we visited the farm to steal maize cobs. There was part of the school that was left wild and that is where we were allowed to cook our own food on Saturday. That is where we roasted our stolen maize and some girls met their boyfriends from the local boarding school. I must have been 15 years when boys from a local boarding school invited some girls to Gary Glitter's show in Bulawayo. One of the girls was my friend and invited me to join them. He was playing on a Saturday evening and a group of us girls joined the boys outside the school along the main road to Bulawayo, an hour's drive to see his show. We were going to watch the show and hitch hike back. I didn't have any money for the show, but I went with them anyway. We left around 9 pm when we knew the nuns were not going to visit our dormitories and the boys were waiting for us in the main road. I think we were 10 altogether and started walking towards Bulawayo. Not a single car stopped despite our frantic waving of hands. After an hour's walk we gave up and walked back to school. The thought that had we been caught, we would have been expelled only crossed my mind as I crawled back into my bed. Nothing was ever said about it to anyone and we never spoke about the experience either. I'm sure we all felt so stupid.

Sundays were very special to most girls as religion was part of our growing up. Nearly all girls who were accepted to the boarding school were accepted because their parents attended the Salvation Army church. We all wore our Sunday uniform and a white beret. We were in church until lunch time and I personally looked forward to Sunday roast. Our menu throughout the week was pretty basic, comprising mainly of paps with milk/beans/cabbage apart from Sunday lunch when we had Sunday roast. My friend Lucy and I would go back to the kitchen after lunch hoping that her uncle who was the school cook would give us left over's. Sometime we were lucky and he would sneak whatever was left over into Lucy's bag. When we found out that at the local boarding school for white girls they had a menu to choose from we went on a demonstration. It was in the evening during study period that we started banging our desk demanding to be given a menu like the girls. We got a beating from the nuns but the menu got a bit better after that.

That was an experience that made me question many things about religion. I had become a zealous Christian who studied the bible as part of the syllabus. I found many contradictions between the teachings in the bible and the reality that we lived, yet we were not allowed to question anything. I enjoyed singing in church, I enjoyed reading the bible during Scripture Union, enjoyed the whole part of being a devout Christian and hoped that as I grew older, things would make sense about this god who lives in heaven. The spiritual part of the bible for me was in the New Testament and I aspired to be a good Christian. However, today I look back at the flaws of the whole book and its contradictions and realise that the spiritual part of the bible is not in the bible. It is living a life that reflects those teachings in the New Testament.

Today I understand racism in a different context. We didn't call it racism from the experience we had as black students who were treated differently from white students. We just knew that it was wrong and against the teachings of Jesus. Today I understand racism from a different context because I understand the origins of racism and segregation. When Professor Steven Hawkins was asked whether he believed in the existence of aliens, his reply was: "A visit from aliens would be like Christopher Columbus arriving in America, which did not turn out very well with the Native Americans." The same scenario in Southern Africa was the arrival of Cecil John Rhodes who displaced black people from their homes, stole their land and livestock, enslaved indigenous people and destroyed our culture and religion played a pivotal role in the creation of racism and oppression of indigenous people.

The creation of the "white race" gave birth to racism by creating an inferior other based on nothing but skin colour. Yet we were all praying to the same god and reading the same bible. The institutionalization of racism was evident in the segregation of black girls from white girls, attending different schools so that white girls can enjoy the benefit of being a white person, and having a menu to choose from.

Chapter 7

There was a local Primary school that was part of the boarding school. It catered mainly for children of farm labourers and local people. We had little interaction with them but my friend Lucy knew some of the children as she was also from a family of farm labourers. In my third year I excelled in my bible studies I was made a Sunday school teacher. Local children attended their own Sunday church at their Primary School and that is where I was allocated as a Sunday school teacher before going to church. I have fond memories of those children, their torn dirty clothes, starvation written on their faces. There I was telling them about the kingdom of God and that Jesus loves them. I had travelled their journey and understood their predicament, but at that age I was still living my indoctrinated life. Somewhere during that period I started to question this whole heaven and hell theory. If sinners truly suffered in hell, then poor people were already in hell. My role as a Sunday school teacher was soon terminated when I asked one of the white nuns why my poor black people were suffering whilst white people lived in comfort. If God truly loved all of us why are poor black people suffering. Her response enraged me even though I didn't show my anger. "God is punishing your people for the sins your ancestors committed." She couldn't hide her anger and disappointment in me and I got punished for it. There were many other incidents when I was punished for not being an obedient Christian girl. I did however finish my "O Levels" with a first in Bible studies and did well in all other subjects.

Before the end of our last year we had a visit from external advisors who came to speak to us about our career prospects. If I remember well, we were put in two groups. This was according to how we performed at school and our predicted final results. I was in group two which was also the largest. A nurse and a teacher spoke to us about their respective careers and how to go about applying for training. Out of the first group I heard that two girls got scholarships to study in Canada. I don't know what happened to others apart from one that I met later on: she had done her "A" levels at a school in Bulawayo and was training as a pharmacist. I had always dreamt of working in a business environment; but nursing and teaching were the only options for black girls in an apartheid racist country. I had outgrown my pubescent years and yet did not have an idea of what to do after completing my "0" Levels. I know Lucy trained as a teacher and taught at the Primary school next to our boarding school. I lost contact with all my peers and had no help from anyone.

One of my cousins got me a job in a clothes factory and I only lasted a couple of months. I couldn't handle the "Yes boss" "No boss" "Thanks boss" kind of environment. I finally got a job working as a temporary teacher in one of the most remote parts of Matebeleland and it was also a haven for freedom fighters. Some schools were raided and older students and teachers taken by guerrillas to join the guerrilla movement that was fighting against the racist regime of Ian Douglas Smith. I utilized that period studying English and Geography at "A" level through correspondence. I only met my lecturer once a month to hand in my assignments and collect my study material. I was determined to not just end up being a teacher or a nurse and hoped that I would be accepted for some Business degree of one form or another. Our school was fortunate enough not to have been visited by the freedom fighters, so we did not have a visit from the Smith soldiers. However, many older students exiled themselves and joined the liberation movement in Zambia. But one day we had a visit from Smith's soldiers and many teachers were taken in for questioning. None that I know of were arrested but news soon spread that these soldiers were torturing teachers in the neighbouring schools. Many teachers including the headmaster left the school and I found another temporary teaching job near my village. This was the time when the rebel in me was born as I saw the abuse my people endured. Unlike the experiences and punishments I got at boarding school for questioning racism, these white soldiers were killing black people they suspected of supporting the freedom fighters in the most brutal manner.

After receiving my "A" level results, I went to stay with my brother Mike in a town where he worked as an Agricultural office. My aim was to find a job. He was already holding a position of power in the agricultural office that he worked at. Many white people were leaving the country in fear of the freedom fighters. My brother told me that one of the white clerks had left and told me to apply for her position. I went to his work place very optimistic as they were looking for a clerk. But when I got to the reception, a white receptionist didn't bother looking at my certificate but turned round and asked her colleagues whether anyone was looking for a nanny. I was not disappointment, but I was enraged and didn't even know what to say to her. I went back to my brother's house fuming and totally besides myself. All that effort and all that hard work to get a good education and still I was just suitable for a nanny's job in my own country. I knew I had to leave the country and I didn't wait for my brother to come home. I packed a little bag with my clothes, took some coins from my brother's jacket and I hitch hiked from Gwelo to Bulawayo and spent a night at my aunt's house in Mzilikazi but never told them where I was going. I left Bulawayo around noon and hitch hiked to Plumtree: I travelled nearly 300 km distance on my own, hitch hiking and telling drivers some soapy stories about why I was travelling and that I had no money until I crossed the border between Rhodesia and Botswana on my own. I was 17 years of age.

The year before at the age of 16, I threw my Gideon bible into a flooded river near my home and cursed the God who justified the suffering of my people. As I crossed the border, I left behind my childhood memories and dreamt of getting a better education so as to come back as an educated woman capable to work in an office and earning a reasonable wage so as help my people. Not only did I leave behind my childhood memories, but I also lost my purity of innocence as I embarked on a ruthless world of living in exile. As in the words of Aeschylus; "I know how people in exile feed on dreams." The childhood memories were soon overtaken by dreams and fears: will I ever get the right education and will I ever go back to my liberated home and help my village. I missed my mother and everything I held dear growing up in my village. I wondered whether my brother Mike would ever forgive me for leaving without even explaining to him why I left and how the job interview had gone. Was my brother angry with me or was I angry with myself for that haste decision that was now irreversible. Once in exile, you couldn't go back as there was no communication between Rhodesia and Zambia. Besides you would end up being killed by either freedom fighters who would regard you as a traitor or by the Smith regime. I wondered how my mother was coping but I couldn't even write her a letter as I did when I was at boarding school. It was a very crude awakening for me as my expectations were different from the reality. I expected to go to school straight away. But I was in the camp with hundreds of other young ladies enduring endless military training for 6 months. Within those 6 months there was a functional normality of some sort, like a prisoner in a maximum prison. I knew both my parents and my brother were heartbroken. All I wished for was to tell them that I was still alive.

Chapter 8

My Parents

I still keep my childhood and family memories alive because they make me who I am. But today I can stand back and look at my memories without yearning to live in them. I accept that things end, people die, relationships end, people change but memories last forever. I look back and see how my childhood memories were the foundation that made me who I am, unforgettable memories. As in the words of Corrie Boom, My childhood memories are truly the key not the past, but to the future. As much as it was hard for me to move on because of regrets for not having fulfilled my village dreams, I took with me the best memories that have nurtured me through life's trials and tribulations and writing journals about my childhood was also a blessing and I revisit one I wrote for my mother:

SOME MOTHERS ARE HARD TO
FORGET 30th July 2011

A thank you letter to my mother.

I took the lessons and the punishment just as you taught me. I applied them in real life, paid the price but I have triumphed – thank you mama. You were the disciplinarian in our family and your word was final. When I came home crying for being punished by the nuns for asking them a question as to why they were rich and my people poor, you encouraged me to question authority and take punishment for it. When I recounted a story I had heard from a friend, you demanded to know whether I had checked the authenticity of the story before repeating it. When it turned out to be untrue, you got annoyed with me and told me never to believe lies. Your words were simple: "Before you open your mouth, ask yourself this question; "Why am I saying this?" Before you believe what someone tells you, ask yourself this question; "Why are they telling me this?" You hated gossip with passion and your friends trusted your judgment. I so much looked up to you and never imagined a day when you would not be in my life. No wonder why darkness took over my life when you said goodbye to this world: that day in October 1981 left me directionless, lost in the maze of life, but I continued to fight my battles just as you taught me. I found myself alone in my battles, my battles for truth. It will be thirty years this October since you have been gone, yet I know that despite feeling alone, you are always here with me. It is time to say a special 'thank you' to you mama, my friend, my teacher and my angel.

As a mother myself, I would have loved to share my parental skill with you mama. But I am sharing them with the universe, because from the universe you came to be my mother and to teach me these wonderful lessons. I often speak to myself and some of the questions I ask are: Mothers, what do you do if your child tells lies about another child? What do you do if your child deliberately hurts another child? What do you do if your child steals from another person or from you? Children, what do you learn from your mothers? Are you like your parents and do you do what they taught you or what you saw them do? Whatever your answers are, let me tell you about the strength of the bond between me and my mother and between me and my son. My mother guided me in her physical life and still does in her spiritual life. Without her guidance, I would be dead, killed by children whose parents taught them that it is okay to hate others, to hurt those you hate and that it is okay to steal. Some of these people with this mentality might have been brought up by honest loving parents, but somewhere in their development, they became self-made monsters. I have no doubt that despite talking to myself, the universe hears me just as prayer is heard by God.

By the mid-1990s my father had outlived all his friends and it was obvious he was no longer comfortable socialising with the younger generation. He died in 2003, 22 years after the death of my mother. Until his death, I maintained my yearly visit to my village to visit him. It was the highlight of all my holidays because every time I visited, he performed his African ancestral celebration to welcome me home. I used to fill my hired car with groceries for my village people to share and my step mother brewed umqomboti (African beer). The celebrations were held yearly to appease my father's ancestors. People danced, ate and drank until the early hours of the morning. The following day, my father and I always went for a walk around our village where we talked about my mother. He always talked about how our village had changed as all his friends were dead. On my visit in 1998 he told me that he wanted to visit England just to see how we lived. He had no passport, so I applied a passport for him before I left. I bought him the ticket and he visited me in August 1999. He brought with him some ingredients to brew umqomboti and he helped me brew it as I had never done that before. On the 7th day he asked me to put some umqomboti in a container and told me that he wanted to do his ancestral ritual for me. He asked me to find a secluded place where no one would disturb us. The two of us walked to some secluded part of Swanscombe Peninsula, a mile from my house. We set under a tree, and he started talking to his ancestors whilst pouring umqomboti around an oak tree. It was an amazing experience for me just to see my father's unconditional love and how much sadness he too must have carried on his own. He asked his ancestors to look after me when he is gone and thanked them for blessing him with a kind and compassionate daughter. After his death, I had to re-evaluate the meaning of my life because the dream I had for my village refused to die. But I knew I was going to go for it alone driven by this urge to keep the legacy of these two wonderful people I was blessed as parents alive. To be blessed with such wonderful parents is truly a divine gift:

Looking back at my childhood 40 years later, I am left with a deep sense of nostalgia for the long – distance way of life; the tranquillity and sense of belonging that is sadly missing today.

From the time I left home as a 17 year – old who had not only lost her belief in the bible, but would also lose my mother and brother, the two people who anchored my life and who I was, I spent many years searching for my place in this world; searching for a way of life that had meaning and spoke of who I was. I had attached who I was to the dream I shared with my brother of helping my people and my village to who Florence was and what her role is in this world. And when that dream fell apart with the death of my father in 2003, I was left with a deep-seated identity crisis and completely disconnected from my past. It was only when I started having dreams and nightmares that forced me to reconnect with my childhood memories that I started on my journey which would bring me to the

Florence that I am today. Even though I have lost the most important people in my life, people who I loved dearly and who anchored me; and even though the childhood dream that I had nursed and worked hard for fell apart, and the unhappy realisation that the village I grew up is no longer the place I call home, the memories of my childhood I recaptured in this book not only allowed me to reconnect with a sense of self that allows me to walk proudly in this world, but they taught me an important lesson: the memories we carry of where we come from and who we are, and by their very existence, our sense of identity do not belong to a place, but rather they live in us.

---

[1]. Hennie P. P. Lötter: Injustice, Violence and Peace

www.ingramcontent.com/pod-product-compliance
Lightning Source LLC
Chambersburg PA
CBHW021159080526
44588CB00008B/415